DISCOVER & LEARN

ANIMAL CLASSIFICATION

by
Steffi Cavell-Clarke
& Charlie Ogden

Photocredits
Abbreviations: l-left, r-right, b-bottom, t-top, c-centre, m-middle.

Front Cover - Aleksey Stemmer. 2 - D'July. 4tl - PhotoSky. 4tm - taviphoto. 4tr - Eric Isselee. 4b - Shchipkova Elena. 5 - Travel landscapes background. 6 - Maggy Meyer. 7t - Tei Sinthip. 7b - Sanne vd Berg Fotografie. 8 - Canon Boy. 9 - Seb c'est bien. 10 - javarman. 11tr - Smileus. 11tl - nattanan726. 11br - Eric Isselee. 11bl - Rudmer Zwerver. 12 - Edwin Butter. 13 - Andreas R.. 14 - davemhuntphotography. 15 - Brandon Alms. 16 - Dirk Ercken. 17 - Rosa Jay. 18 - Shane Gross. 19 - Vangert. 19inset - Hintau Aliaksei. 20 - Willyam Bradberry. 21 - Jacqueline Lee. 22 - RZwa. 23 - Lee319. 24 - Neale Cousland. 25 - Martin Mecnarowski. 26 - Ondrej Prosicky. 27 - Kletr. 28 - Christian Vinces. 29 - Sebastian Janicki. 30 - FikMik. Images are courtesy of Shutterstock.com. With thanks to Getty Images, Thinkstock Photo and iStockphoto.

Book Life
King's Lynn
Norfolk PE30 4LS

ISBN: 978-1-78637-154-6

Printed in Malaysia

A catalogue record for this book
is available from the British Library.

Written by:
Steffi Cavell-Clarke
Charlie Ogden

Designed by:
Drue Rintoul
Natalie Carr

CONTENTS

Words in **bold** are explained in the glossary on page 31.

THE ANIMAL KINGDOM

The animal kingdom includes over 8 million known living **species**. They come in many different shapes and sizes, they each do weird and wonderful things and they live all over planet Earth.

From the freezing Arctic waters to the hottest desert in the world, animals have **adapted** to the often extreme and diverse conditions upon Earth.

Even though each and every species of animal is **unique**, they still share certain **traits** with each other. These shared traits are used to group animals. There are six main groups of animal classification.

- Mammals
- Reptiles
- Amphibians
- Fish
- Birds
- Insects

Roughly 10,000 new species of animal are discovered every year.

MAMMALS

WHAT IS A MAMMAL?

A mammal is a type of animal that breathes air using lungs, has a backbone and usually grows fur on its body. Most mammals give birth to live young and produce milk to feed them. Mammals are warm-blooded animals, which means that their body temperature stays the same, even if they live in a very hot or very cold **habitat**.

MAMMAL CHECKLIST:

- Give birth to live young
- Produce milk to feed their young
- Usually have fur on their bodies
- Warm-blooded
- Breathe using lungs
- **Vertebrate**

BODY PARTS

Mammals come in lots of different shapes and sizes, which can sometimes make it difficult to work out whether an animal is a mammal or not! However, there are a few traits that all mammals share. One example of a mammal that has all of these traits is a dog. Female dogs also have mammary glands, which produce milk that they use to feed their young.

EXTREME MAMMALS

BROWN BEAR

Every autumn, brown bears will start to eat as much food as they can find. This gives the bear a thick layer of fat that it can survive on for the entire winter. In October or November, the brown bear will crawl into a hole or a cave and fall asleep for the next four to seven months. This process is called hibernation.

SIZE:
Up to 3 metres long

HOME:
Forests and mountains in North America, northern Europe and northern Asia

DIET:
Fruit, roots and fish

During hibernation, a bear's heartbeat becomes very slow and it can lose up to 40% of its body weight.

HUMPBACK WHALE

Humpback whales make the longest **migration** of any mammal in the world. These whales spend most of their time in cold Arctic waters, but during the winter they swim 5000 miles to warmer waters. However, individual humpback whales have been known to make journeys nearly twice this length!

SIZE:
16 metres long

HOME:
Warm, shallow ocean waters

DIET:
Krill and small fish

REPTILES

WHAT IS A REPTILE?

There are over 9,000 different species of reptile in the world. Each species is different and they all have individual features that help them to survive in their habitats. Reptiles have backbones and their skin is almost completely covered in scales.

Reptiles usually live on land, but some, such as turtles and crocodiles, can also live in water. Reptiles are cold-blooded animals, which means that the body temperature of a reptile changes depending on the temperature of its environment.

REPTILE CHECKLIST:

- Usually lay eggs
- Breathe using lungs
- Skin covered in scales
- Cold-blooded
- Vertebrate

BODY PARTS

Even though all species of reptile are unique, they can still be grouped together using their shared characteristics. Each class of animal can be broken down into smaller groups called 'orders'. Animals in the same order are even more similar to one another than those in the same class. The class of reptile has four main orders.

TORTOISES AND TURTLES

Tortoises and turtles have bony shells on their backs that are covered in horny plates called scutes. Many species in this order can hide in their shells when they sense danger.

CROCODILES AND ALLIGATORS

Crocodiles and alligators are large reptiles with powerful jaws and tails. They spend most of their time in water.

SNAKES AND LIZARDS

Snakes are reptiles that have long, flexible bodies and no legs. Lizards have four **limbs** and a tail. Some lizards have long tongues that they use to catch **prey**.

TUATARAS

Tuataras have spiky scales, called spines, down the centre of their backs and look very similar to lizards.

EXTREME REPTILES

GALÁPAGOS GIANT TORTOISE

The Galápagos tortoise is the largest species of tortoise on the planet. It is only found on the Galápagos Islands in the Pacific Ocean. They are extremely peaceful creatures and they like to spend their days eating grass and leaves. They also sleep for nearly 16 hours every day! Their huge bodies can store large amounts of water, which means that they can survive for up to a year without eating or drinking.

SIZE:
1.5 metres long
HOME:
Galápagos Islands
DIET:
Plants and fruit

The oldest Galápagos tortoise that ever lived reached 175 years old!

KOMODO DRAGON

The Komodo dragon is a huge reptile that lives on Indonesian islands. Komodo dragons are the world's heaviest lizards and they are deadly **predators**. They will eat almost anything they find, including deer, fish and even humans! When a Komodo spots its prey, it springs into action and uses its sharp claws to hold the animal down. A quick bite with its sharp teeth allows the Komodo to pass **venom** into its prey. The Komodo dragon does this because if the prey escapes, the venom will weaken it, meaning that the Komodo dragon will probably be able to catch the prey again and finish its meal.

SIZE:
3 metres long

HOME:
Grasslands on Indonesian islands

DIET:
Large and small animals, even humans

AMPHIBIANS

WHAT IS AN AMPHIBIAN?

An amphibian is a type of animal that lays eggs, has a backbone and has a thin, moist, **permeable** skin. All amphibians are amphibious, which means that they can live on land and in water.

Amphibians are also cold-blooded animals and they can be found in many different types of habitat around the world. Salamanders, newts, frogs and toads are all types of amphibian.

AMPHIBIAN CHECKLIST:

- Lays eggs
- Lives in water and on land
- Thin, moist, permeable skin
- Cold-blooded
- Vertebrate

BODY PARTS

Even though amphibians can look very different from one another, there are certain traits that nearly all species of amphibian share. They have unique skins that help them to survive. An amphibian's skin will usually be permeable, very soft and covered in a thin layer of slime that helps to keep it moist. As well as this, many species of amphibian are able to breathe through their skin both when they are underwater and when they are on land.

EXTREME AMPHIBIANS

GLASS FROG

The glass frog of Central and South America has very thin skin. In fact, the skin on its **abdomen** is so thin that it is actually transparent, meaning that you can see through it! These tiny frogs spend a lot of their time in trees trying to stay hidden from predators.

Because of this, scientists believe that the glass frog's transparent skin may help it to blend in with its environment and escape being eaten by larger animals. However, all we know for certain is that this is one of the most unusual amphibians on the planet.

SIZE:
3–7.5 cm long
HOME:
Forests in Central and South America
DIET:
Spiders and insects

LONG-NOSED HORNED FROG

The long-nosed horned frog is a unique looking frog species that has developed large, horn-shaped pieces of skin above its eyes and snout. As well as this, the long-nosed horned frog also has folds in the skin on its back and sides. The unusual look of this frog helps it to blend in with leaves and sticks on the forest floor. This allows the long-nosed horned frog to wait, hidden amongst the leaves, until a spider or lizard moves close enough to grab!

SIZE:
10–12 cm long

HOME:
Rainforests in Southeast Asia

DIET:
Spiders, lizards, mice and other frogs

FISH

WHAT IS A FISH?

There are over 30,000 known species of fish alive today. A fish is a type of animal that has a **streamline** body as well as a backbone, gills and fins. All fish must live in water in order to survive. Most fish are cold-blooded and covered in scales. However, there are also a few exceptions! Overall, there are six characteristics that nearly all fish have in common.

Fish include sharks, rays, salmon and perch.

FISH CHECKLIST:

- Live in water
- Scaly skin
- Breathe through gills
- Fins
- Cold-blooded
- Vertebrate

BODY PARTS

Fish have several fins that help them to move and steer through the water. The skin of a fish is often covered in scales. Scales are overlapping pieces of bone-like material that form a protective layer around the fish's body.

All fish have gills that allow them to breathe underwater. Gills are **organs** that are usually located on either side of a fish's head. As water flows over the gills, **oxygen** from the water passes into the fish's **bloodstream**.

EXTREME FISH

GREAT WHITE SHARK

All species of shark are **carnivores**. Because of this, many species of shark spend most of their time looking for and hunting prey. The great white shark has developed very powerful senses that help it to find its prey. It uses a unique sensor system located in its nose. This system means that great white sharks can detect even the smallest movements in the water, even fish lying under the sand!

SIZE:
6.4 m long
HOME:
Coastal areas
DIET:
Fish, rays, seals and other sharks

LEAFY SEADRAGON

The leafy seadragon gets its name from the flaps of skin that cover its body and look like seaweed. As it moves though the water, the skin flaps drift behind it, making it look similar to a piece of floating seaweed. This amazing form of **camouflage** helps the leafy seadragon to stay hidden, even as it drifts through open waters. They also have a long, straw-like mouth for sucking up tiny shrimps.

SIZE:
24 cm long
HOME:
Off the southern and western coasts of Australia
DIET:
Shrimps, sea lice and fish fry

BIRDS

WHAT IS A BIRD?

A bird is a type of animal that lays hard-shelled eggs and has a backbone, feathers and a hard beak. All birds have wings and most birds use them to fly. However, some species of bird are flightless, meaning that they cannot fly. Birds also have a unique way of breathing. They have organs called air sacs that push the air in and out of their bodies.

Birds have between seven and eleven air sacs in their bodies, depending on what species they are.

BIRD CHECKLIST:

- Lay hard-shelled eggs
- Have wings, feathers and beaks
- Most can fly
- Warm-blooded
- Vertebrate

BODY PARTS

Different species of bird can look very different from one another. However, there are some body parts that all birds have. We use these common traits to work out which animals are birds and which are not. All birds have a light skeleton, two wings, two legs, a beak and feathers all over their body. Also, birds always lay eggs instead of giving birth to live young.

EXTREME BIRDS

EMPEROR PENGUIN

Lots of different birds can swim; however, none can swim as well as the emperor penguin. Like other penguins, the emperor penguin has developed wings and feet that are brilliant at pushing the bird through the water. However, the emperor penguin is special in that it can dive up to 1,500 feet deep. That's more than the height of the Empire State Building and seven times deeper than most other penguins can dive.

SIZE: 120 cm tall
HOME: Antarctica
DIET: Fish

HUMMINGBIRD

Hummingbirds are able to move backwards or even hover in the same place when they fly, almost like they are floating. They are able to do this because their wings flap up to 4,200 times every minute. Flapping their wings so fast uses a lot of energy and means that a hummingbird can die in only a few hours if it doesn't eat. Because of this, hummingbirds often eat twice their own bodyweight in nectar in a single day.

SIZE:
5–13 cm long
HOME:
North America, South America and the Caribbean
DIET:
Nectar

INSECTS

WHAT IS AN INSECT?

Insects are part of a larger group of animals called invertebrates, which are animals that don't have skeletons or backbones. Other invertebrates include octopuses, snails and tarantulas. Instead of having a skeleton, most insects have an exoskeleton, which is a hard, outer shell that supports and protects the animal's body. Insects also have long antennae on their heads that they use to sense heat, movement, smells and taste.

INSECT CHECKLIST:

- Three-part body
- Three pairs of legs
- **Compound eyes**
- Antennae
- Exoskeleton
- Invertebrate

BODY PARTS

Even though many species of insect can look very different from one another, there are certain traits that all species of insect share. All insects have three body sections; the head, the thorax and the abdomen.

An insect's compound eyes and antennae are found on its head, while the thorax is where the legs and the wings are located. The abdomen is the part of the body that contains the insect's organs.

EXTREME INSECTS

BULLET ANT

Some insects have developed powerful weapons to use against anything that might try to attack or eat them. One such insect is the venomous bullet ant, who has one of the most painful venoms in the entire animal kingdom. These ants have developed a powerful venom in order to be able to protect themselves from larger predators who might not react to a weaker venom. The sting is so painful that some have said that it feels like being shot, which is why they are called bullet ants.

SIZE:
Up to 2.5 cm long

HOME:
Forests and jungles in Central and South America

DIET:
Nectar and smaller insects

Although the bullet ant has one of the strongest venoms in the animal kingdom, it is actually a very calm animal that won't attack unless it is provoked.

WALKING FLOWER MANTIS

Rather than develop a venom in order to attack other animals, some insects prefer to stay out of sight until just the right moment. Walking flower mantises are a species of mantis that are able to camouflage themselves extremely well. They have adapted to be brightly coloured and have large **appendages** that make them look exactly like flowers. Walking flower mantises use their amazing ability to blend in with flowers in order to stay out of sight until an insect comes close enough to grab!

SIZE:
Up to 6 cm long
HOME:
Rainforests in Southeast Asia
DIET:
Insects, especially moths and butterflies

FIND OUT MORE

BOOKS

Amphibians (Living Things & Their Habitats) by Grace Jones (BookLife, 2016)

Birds (Living Things & Their Habitats) by Grace Jones (BookLife, 2016)

Fish (Living Things & Their Habitats) by Grace Jones (BookLife, 2016)

Insects (Living Things & Their Habitats) by Grace Jones (BookLife, 2017)

Mammals (Living Things & Their Habitats) by Grace Jones (BookLife, 2016)

Reptiles (Living Things & Their Habitats) by Grace Jones (BookLife, 2017)

WEBSITES

WWF

www.wwf.org.uk

On this website you can follow links to information on all sorts of animals and find out what WWF is doing to save wildlife around the world.

BBC NATURE

www.bbc.co.uk/nature

Discover all the different species of animal and their different types of habitat.

GLOSSARY

abdomen	the part of the body that contains the reproductive and digestive organs
adapted	changed over time to suit an environment
appendages	projecting parts of invertebrates that have particular functions
bloodstream	the blood that circulates around the body
camouflage	colours, shapes or patterns that help an animal to hide in its environment
carnivores	animals that eat other animals rather than plants
compound eyes	eyes that have multiple lenses
habitat	the natural home or environment of a living thing
limbs	arms, legs and wings
migration	the seasonal movement of animals from one area to another
organs	parts of animals that have specific jobs or functions
oxygen	a gas that all living things need to breathe in order to stay alive
permeable	something that allows liquid or gas to pass through it
predators	animals that hunt prey
prey	animals that are hunted by other animals
species	a group of very similar animals that are capable of producing young together
streamline	a shape that has low resistance in water and air
traits	qualities or characteristics
unique	unlike anything else
venom	a harmful substance that comes from a bite or a sting
vertebrate	an animal with a backbone

INDEX